CAMERON MACKINTOSH

PRESENTS

MISS
Saigon

A MUSICAL BY

ALAIN BOUBLIL & CLAUDE-MICHEL SCHÖNBERG

Music by CLAUDE-MICHEL SCHÖNBERG
Lyrics by RICHARD MALTBY, JR. & ALAIN BOUBLIL
Adapted from original French lyrics by ALAIN BOUBLIL
Additional material by RICHARD MALTBY, JR.

Musical supervision by DAVID CADDICK & MARTIN KOCH
Directed by NICHOLAS HYTNER
Musical staging by BOB AVIAN
Production designed by JOHN NAPIER
Costumes designed by ANDREANE NEOFITOU
Lighting by DAVID HERSEY
Sound by ANDREW BRUCE
Orchestration by WILLIAM D. BROHN

All songs in this edition copyright © 1987, 1988, 1989, 1990 by
Alain Boublil Music Limited
c/o Laventhol & Horwath,
605 Third Avenue, New York, NY10158, USA.
All songs sub-published for the UK & Eire by
Alain Boublil (Overseas) Limited, 8 Baker Street, London W1M 1DA.

Hal Leonard Publishing Corporation
7777 West Bluemound Road P.O. Box 13819 Milwaukee, WI 53213

'This photograph was for Alain and I the start of everything...'

Claude-Michel Schönberg, October 1985

'The heat is on in Saigon
the girls are hotter 'n hell.'

MISS Saigon

The Heat Is On In Saigon
9

The Movie In My Mind
16

Why God Why?
22

Sun And Moon
29

The Last Night Of The World
34

I Still Believe
43

If You Want To Die In Bed
51

I'd Give My Life For You
61

Bui-doi
67

Now That I've Seen Her
formerly 'Her Or Me'
74

The American Dream
79

This book © Copyright 1990.

Rights of dramatic performance for all countries of
the world administered by
Cameron Mackintosh (Overseas) Limited,
1 Bedford Square, London WC1B 3RA.
Telephone: 071-637 8866. Telex: 226164 (CAMACK).
Fax: 071-436 2683.

Photography by Michael Le Poer Trench.
Music arranged by Tony Castro.
Music processed by Barnes Music Engraving.
Cover & logo device design by Dewynters plc.
Cover design Copyright © by Cameron Mackintosh (Overseas) Limited.
Book design by Mike Bell.
Typeset by Capital Setters.

'I have a heart like the sea
million dreams are in me.'

'I'm from a world that's so different
from all that you are
how in the light of one night
did we come so far?'

'In a place that won't let us feel
in a life where nothing seems real
I have found you.'

'This room! This shame
will haunt you while you live.'

'I have killed with this hand,
I have killed oh why am I cold?
For this must be a judgement fulfilled'.

'They're called Bui-doi, the dust of life
conceived in hell and born in strife.'

'We can't forget, must not forget
that they are all our children too.'

'They'll kill who they find here
don't leave us behind here.'

'What's that I smell in the air?
The American dream.'

'As long as you can have your chance
I swear I'll give my life for you.'

The Heat Is On
In Saigon

Music by Claude-Michel Schönberg
Lyrics by Richard Maltby Jr. & Alain Boublil
Adapted from original French Lyrics by Alain Boublil

Americans

The heat is on in Sai-gon ____ the girls are hot-ter 'n Hell

one of these slits here will be Miss Sai-gon God the ten-sion is high

_ not to men-tion the smell _

The heat is on in Sai-gon _ Is there a war go-ing on?

Don't ask I ain't gon-na tell _____

How are you do-ing there John?

I got the hots for Y-vonne

I tell you Bud-dy I've had it   I don't want to hear

We should get drunk and get laid __ since the end is so near __

The heat is on in Sai-gon __ but 'til they tell me I'm gone __ I'm gon-na buy you a girl

You can buy me a beer

gently

p

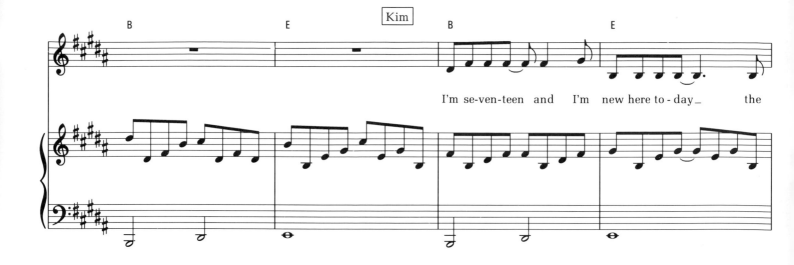

I'm se-ven-teen and I'm new here to-day__ the

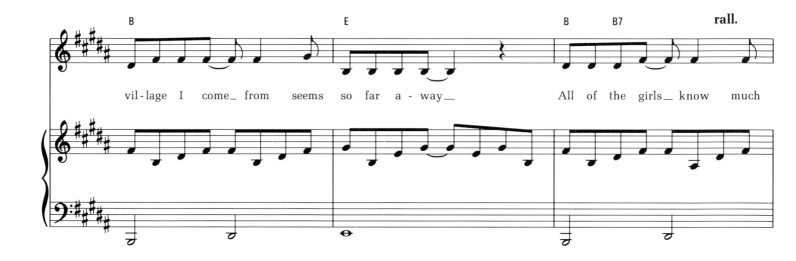

vil-lage I come__ from seems so far a-way__ All of the girls__ know much

more what to say__ but I know I have a heart like the sea_____ A mil-lion dreams are in me

Good Je - sus John who is she?

a tempo

The Cong is tight-'ning the noose___ Is it a week or a day or an hour that we get?

to-night could be our last shot got to put it to use

to-night I bet that you and I will get a - long. For-get a-bout the threat for - get the Vi - et - cong

Mi - mi   Gi - gi   Y - vette or Y - vonne_____   Gon-na buy me a beer

__ and e - lect Miss Sai - gon

(Engineer: Attention s'il vous plaît! By popula

demand, Miss Gigi Van Tranh, is crowned Miss Saigon!)   The heat is on in Sai-gon

and things are not go-ing well   but still at mid-night   the   par-ty goes on —

a good-bye par-ty in hell

The Movie In My Mind

Music by Claude-Michel Schönberg
Lyrics by Richard Maltby Jr. & Alain Boublil
Adapted from original French Lyrics by Alain Boublil

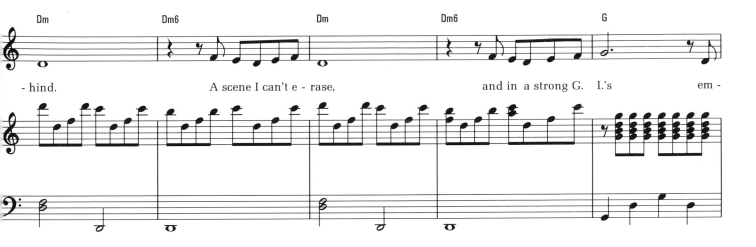

- hind. A scene I can't e - rase, and in a strong G. I.'s em -

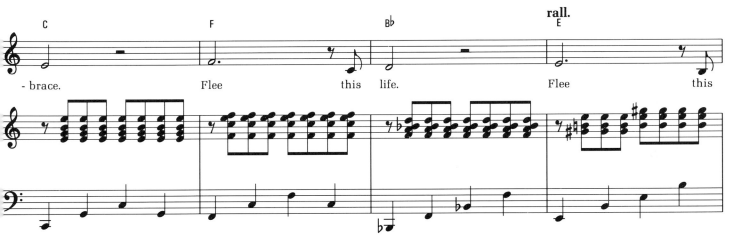

- brace. Flee this life. Flee this

place. The mo-vie plays and plays. The screen be-fore me

fills. He takes me to New York, he gives me dol-lar bills.

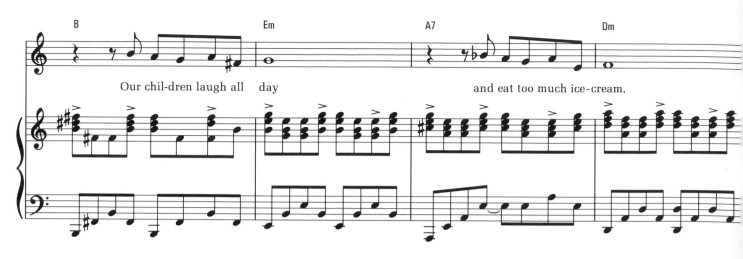

Our chil-dren laugh all day and eat too much ice-cream,

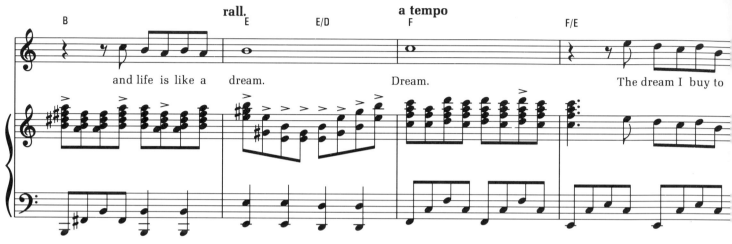

and life is like a dream. Dream. The dream I buy to

find. The mo-vie in my mind._____ I will not cry, I will not

think. I'll do my dance, I'll make them drink. When I make love it won't be

me, and if they hurt me, I'll just close my eyes and see,

Girls

They are not nice, they're most-ly

the mo - vie in my mind.

The dream that fills my

noise. They kill like men, they die like boys.

head. A man who can - not kill,

They give their cash, they keep their hearts.

But ev - 'ry night a - gain it

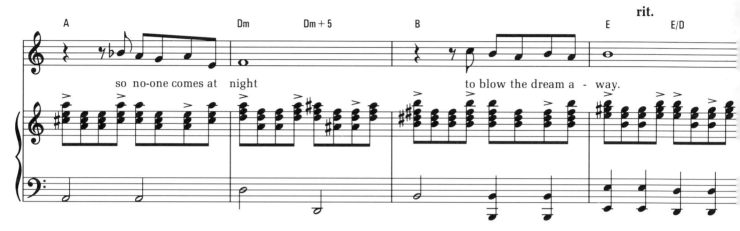

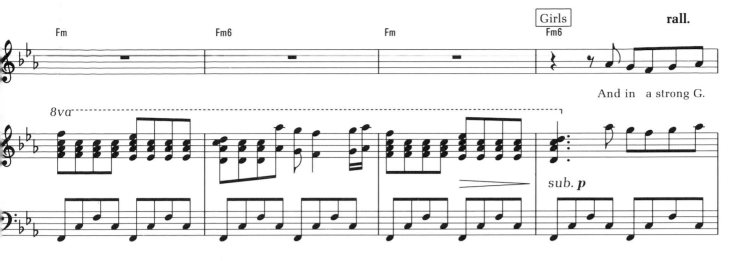

And in a strong G.

I.'s em-brace, flee this life, flee this

place. A world that's far a - way where life is not un -

- kind. The mo-vie in my mind.

Why God Why?

Music by Claude-Michel Schönberg
Lyrics by Richard Maltby Jr. & Alain Boublil
Adapted from original French Lyrics by Alain Boublil

Why is her voice ring-ing in my head? Why am I high on her cheap per-fume. Vi-et-

-nam.___ Hey look I mean you no of-fence, but why does no-thing here make sense.___

Why God? Show your hand. Why can't one_ guy

un-der-stand. I've been with girls who know much more, I ne-ver felt con-fused be-fore.

Why God? What's your plan? I can't help her, no - one can. I liked my mem'-ries as they were but now I'll leave re-mem-b'ring her.

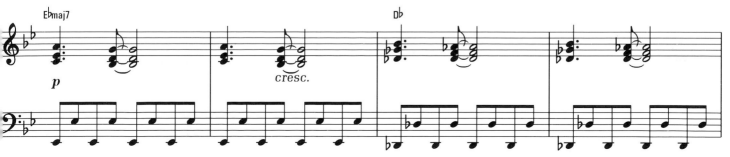

When I went home be - fore____ no - one talked of the war.____ What they knew from T. V.___

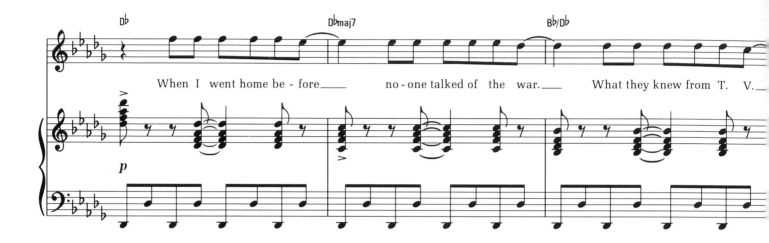

___ did-n't have a thing to do with me.__

I went back and re - upped,__ sure Sai - gon is cor - rupt.__ It felt bet - ter to be__

here dri - ving for the Em - bas - sy.

'Cos here___ if you can pull a string a guy___ like me

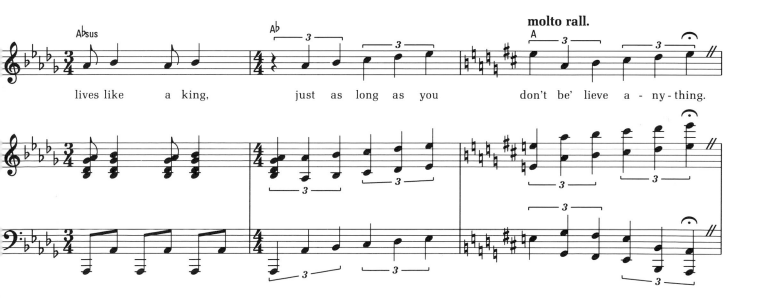

lives like a king, just as long as you don't be' lieve a - ny - thing.

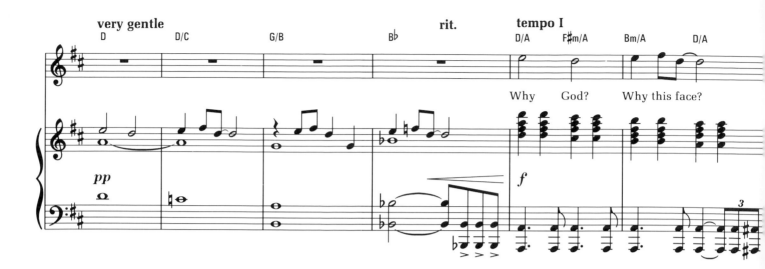

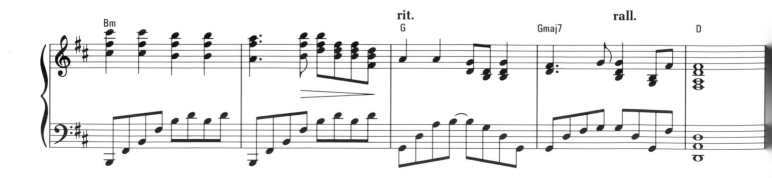

Sun And Moon

Music by Claude-Michel Schönberg
Lyrics by Richard Maltby Jr. & Alain Boublil
Adapted from original French Lyrics by Alain Boublil

and we meet in the sky._____

and we meet in the sky._____

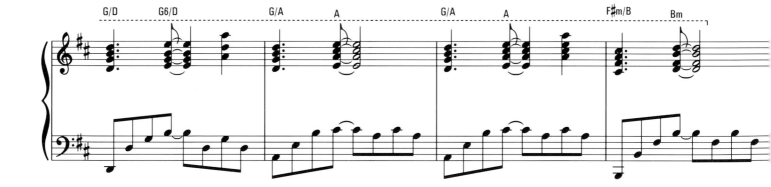

a tempo tranquillo

You are — sun - light and I moon joined here —

bright - 'ning the sky with the flame of love.

Made of — sun - light moon - light.

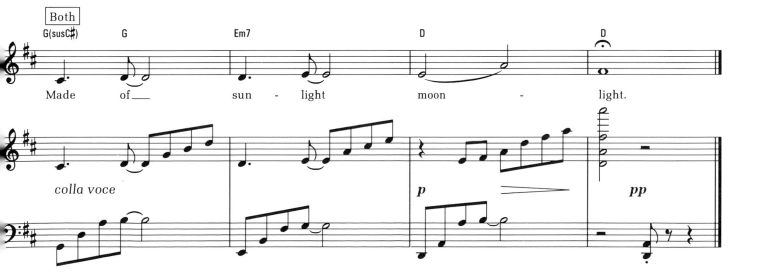

The Last Night Of The World

Music by Claude-Michel Schönberg
Lyrics by Richard Maltby Jr. & Alain Boublil
Adapted from original French Lyrics by Alain Boublil

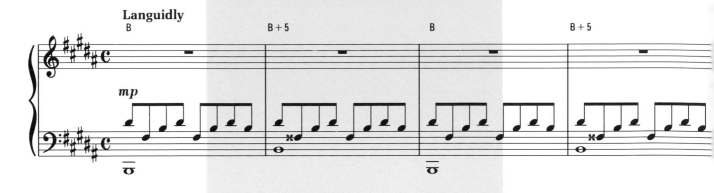

cry   that tells us love___   goes on and on.___   Played on a

cry   that tells us love___   goes on and on.___   Played on a

so - lo sax - o - phone.___   It's tell-ing me___ to hold you tight   and

so - lo sax - o - phone.___   It's tell-ing me___ to hold you tight   and

dance, like it's the last___ night   of the world.

dance, like it's the last___ night   of the world.

If we're to - ge - ther, well then, we'll hear it a - gain. A

If we're to - ge - ther, well then, we'll hear it a - gain. A

song played on a so - lo sax - o - phone,___ a

song played on a so - lo sax - o - phone,___ a

cra - zy sound. A lone - ly sound, a cry that tells us love___ goes on and on.

cra - zy sound. A lone - ly sound, a cry that tells us love___ goes on and on.

Played on a so - lo sax - o - phone.___ It's

Played on a so - lo sax - o - phone.___ It's

tell-ing me___ to hold you tight and dance, like it's the last___ night of the

tell-ing me___ to hold you tight and dance, like it's the last___ night of the

world.___ Dreams___ were all I ev - er knew. Dreams___ you won't need

world.___

Both — E

Chris — A

Kim

when I'm through. A-ny-where we may be I will sing_____ with

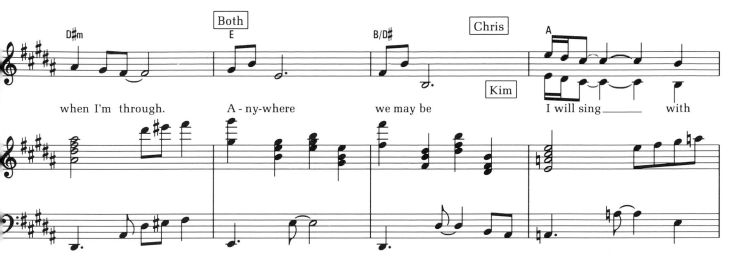

maestoso

you, our song.

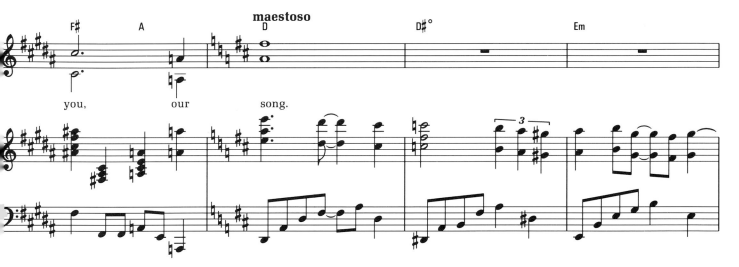

Played on a so - lo sax - o - phone.

Played on a so - lo sax - o - phone.

So stay with me___ and hold me tight___ and dance, like it's the

So stay with me and hold me tight___ and dance, like it's the

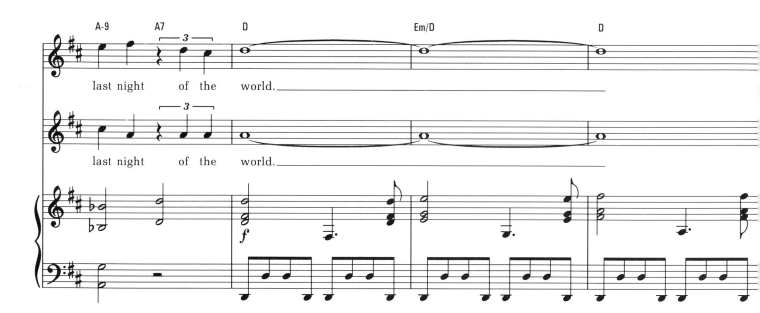

last night of the world.___

last night of the world.___

I Still Believe

Music by Claude-Michel Schönberg
Lyrics by Richard Maltby Jr. & Alain Boublil
Adapted from original French Lyrics by Alain Boublil

Andante con moto

Last night I watched him sleep-ing, my bo-dy pressed to him,

and then he star-ted speak-ing. The name I heard him speak

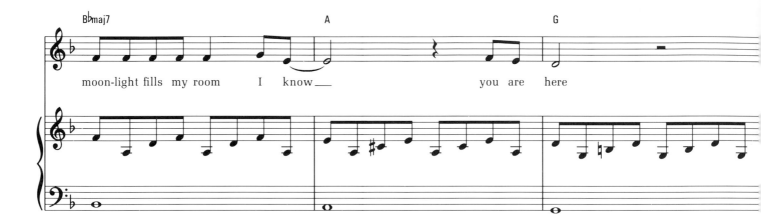

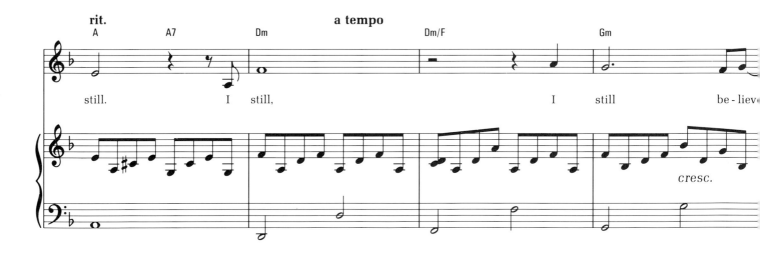

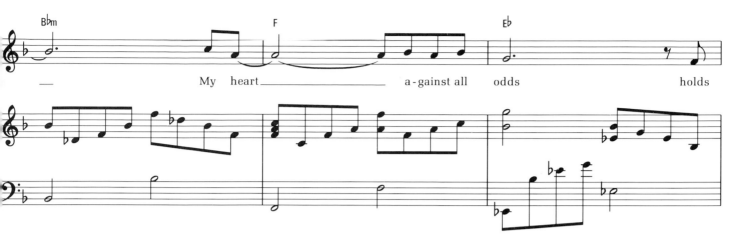

My heart_____ a-gainst all odds_____ holds

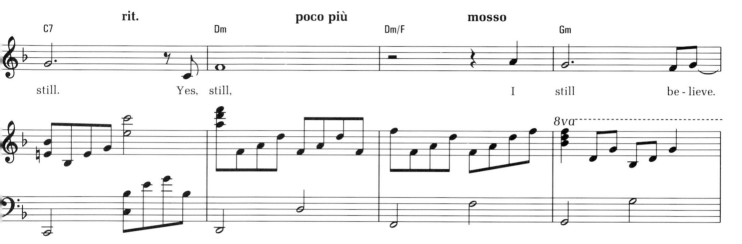

still. Yes, still, I still be-lieve.

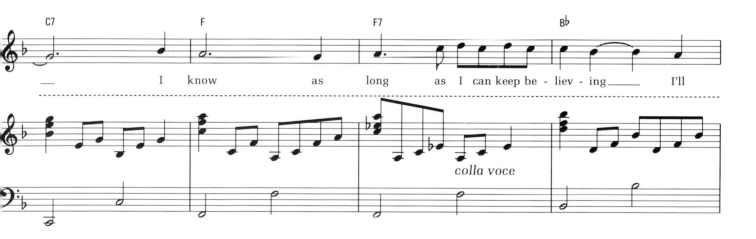

_____ I know as long as I can keep be-liev-ing_____ I'll

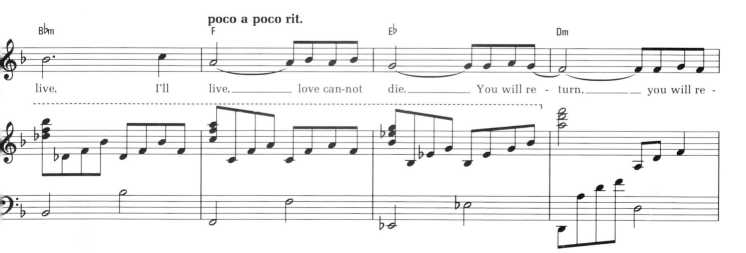

live, I'll live,_____ love can-not die._____ You will re - turn,_____ you will re -

knowing part of you I'll never share,___ never know.___

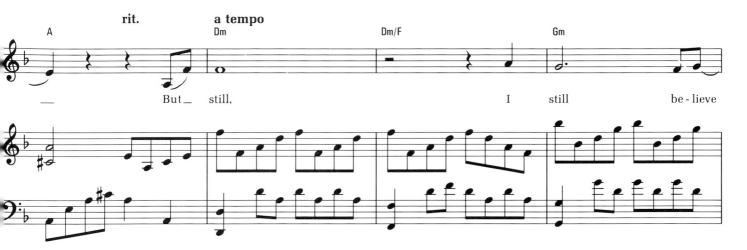

rit. **a tempo**

But___ still, I still be-lieve

poco agitato

the time will come___ when no-thing keeps us a-part.

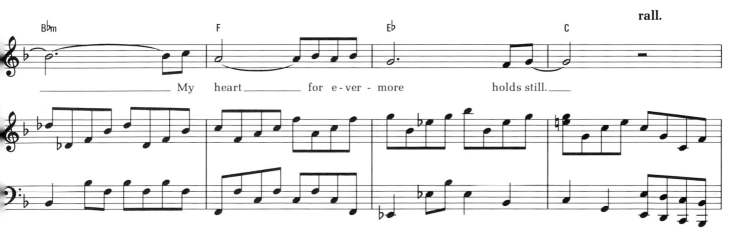

rall.

_____ My heart_____ for e-ver-more holds still.___

It's all o-ver, I'm here, there is no-thing to fear.

Chris, what's haunt - ing

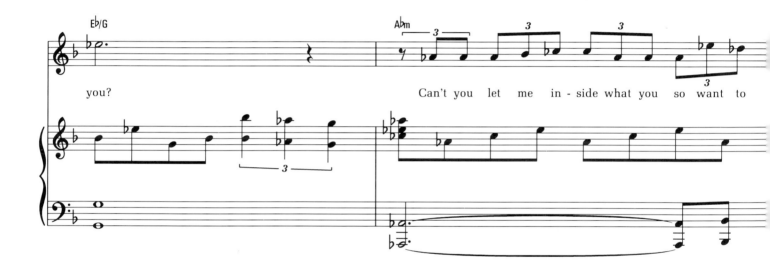

you?

Can't you let me in - side what you so want to

hide.

I need you.

For___

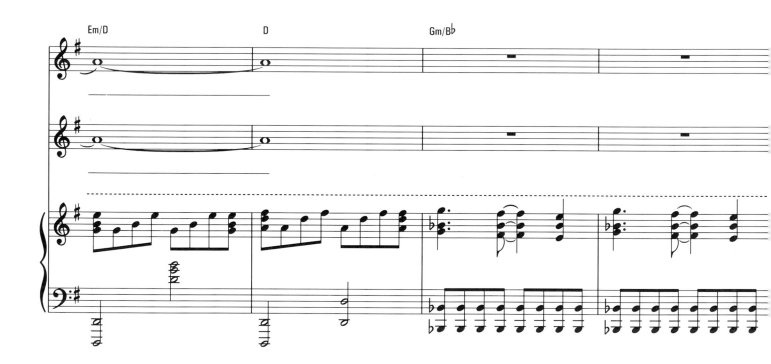

If You Want To Die In Bed

Music by Claude-Michel Schönberg
Lyrics by Richard Maltby Jr. & Alain Boublil
Adapted from original French Lyrics by Alain Boublil

Presto con groove

If you want to die in bed, fol - low my ex - am - ple.

When you see a cloud a - head, it's time__ to show your class.

Hit the door be-fore_____ they make a tar-get of your ass.

If you want to die in bed in times of rev-o-lu-tion,

when the flag they wave is red, let pride_ fill up your chest.

Mean-while pack a sack,____ and take the first boat head-ing

west.

Leggiero, meno mosso

mp

My pre - cious sou - ve - nirs of all___ the gol-den years.

Ro - lex wat-ches in steel___ that look prac-tic-'lly real.___

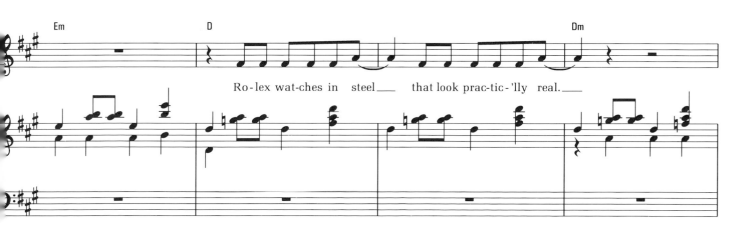

I'll need__ a lit-tle stock to start__ me in Bang-

poco più mosso

-kok. If you want to die in

bed, for-get__ a-bout your Kar - ma.

When your life hangs by a thread, don't cry__ a-bout the fates.

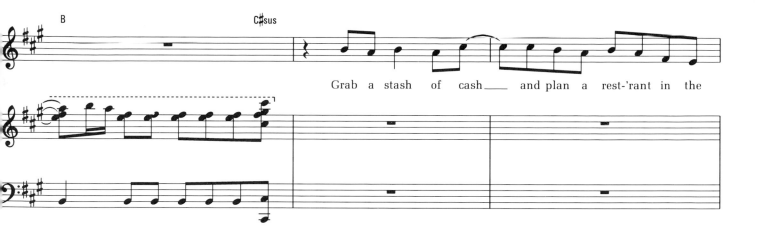

They paid__ me twice, and more for just___ an - o - ther whore.

Here I___ come U. S. A.,

your next__ champ's on his way. For men_____ will al - ways be men,

the rules are the same___ for King or for clerk.___ Show me

francs or dol-lars or yen, I'll set up a game.___ I know how things work.

Why was I born of a race___ that thinks on-ly of rice,___ and hates en-tre-pre-neurs.

Me, I be-long in a place___ where a man sets his price,

_ and you pay and he's yours._

I should be A - mer-i-can_

where ev - 'ry pro-mise lands, and ev - 'ry bus-'ness man knows where he stands.

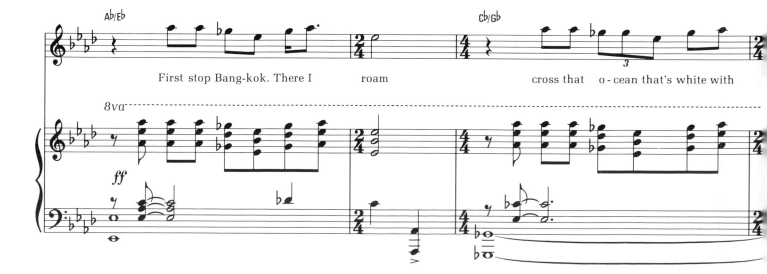

First stop Bang-kok. There I roam cross that o-cean that's white with

foam, to the place that's my heart's true home.

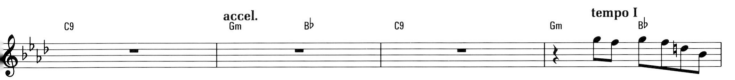

If you want to die in

bed don't care__ too much for coun-try.

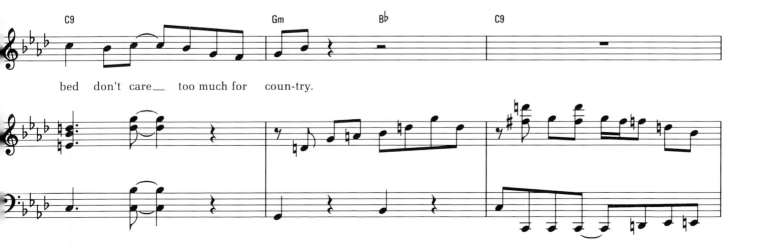

Hit the o-pen sea in-stead and float__ there like a cork.

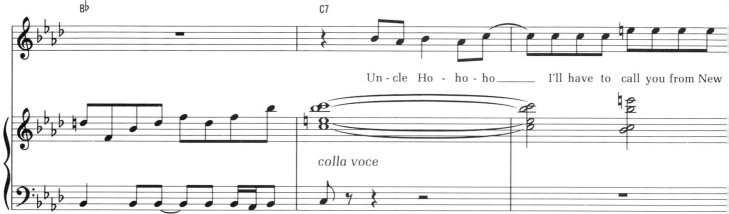

Un-cle Ho - ho - ho_____ I'll have to call you from New

colla voce

York!

ff

I'd Give My Life
For You

Music by Claude-Michel Schönberg
Lyrics by Richard Maltby Jr. & Alain Boublil
Adapted from original French Lyrics by Alain Boublil

You who I cra-dled in my arms. You, ask-ing as lit-tle as you can, ___

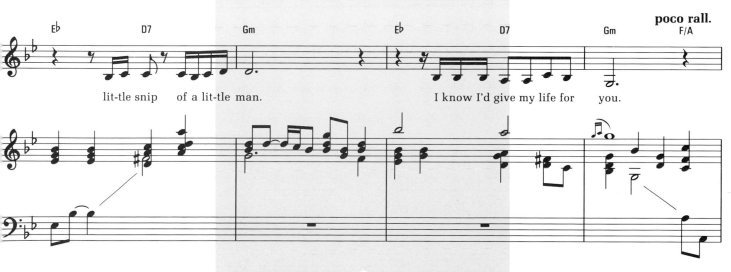

lit-tle snip of a lit-tle man. I know I'd give my life for you.

You did-n't ask me to be born, you. Why should you learn of war or

pain. To make sure you're not hurt a - gain,

I swear I'd give my life for you. I've tast-ed love be-yond all

fear, and you should know it's love that brought you here. And in one per-fect

night,   when the stars burned like new   I knew what I must do.   I'll

give you____ a mil - lion things I'll nev - er own.   I'll

give you____ a world to con - quer when you're   grown.

You will be____ who you want to be.____   You

can choose what ev - er hea - ven

grants,____ as long as you can have a chance.

I swear I'll give my life for you. Some-times I wake up.

Reach-ing for him, I feel his sha-dow brush my head.____

But there's just moon-light on my bed. Was he a ghost, was he a lie?

that made my bo - dy laugh and cry.___ Then by my side the proof I see,___

sub. **p**

molto rall.

his lit - tle one. Gods of the sun___ bring him to

a tempo

me.

You will be who you want to be. You can choose what ev - er hea-ve

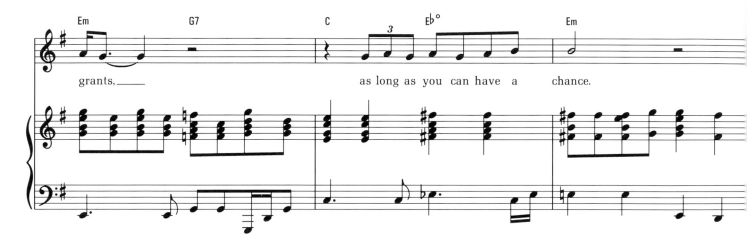

grants,____ as long as you can have a chance.

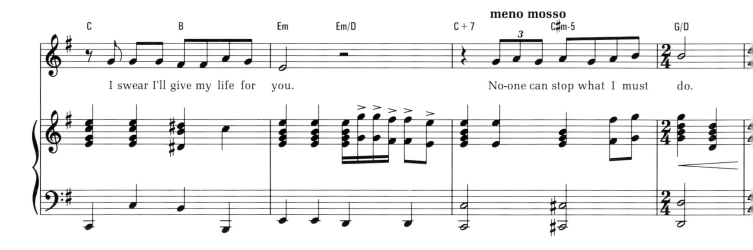

I swear I'll give my life for you. No-one can stop what I must do.

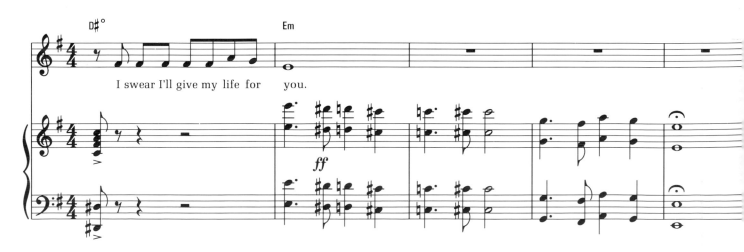

I swear I'll give my life for you.

Bui-doi

Music by Claude-Michel Schönberg
Lyrics by Richard Maltby Jr. & Alain Boublil
Adapted from original French Lyrics by Alain Boublil

Like all sur-vi - vors I once thought when I'm home I won't give a damn, but now__ I know I'm caught. I'll ne-ver leave__ Vi-et - nam. War is-n't o-ver__ when it ends,__ some pic-tures ne-ver leave your mind.

They are the fa - ces of__ the chil - dren, the ones we left be - hind._____ They're called Bu

- doi._____ The dust of life,_____ con - ceived in hell and born in

strife. They are the liv - ing re - min - der of all the good we failed to do. We can't for

- get, must not for - got that they are all our__ chil - dren too.

-dren, whose crime was be-ing born. They're called Bui - doi. The dust of

life, con-ceived in hell and born in strife. We owe them

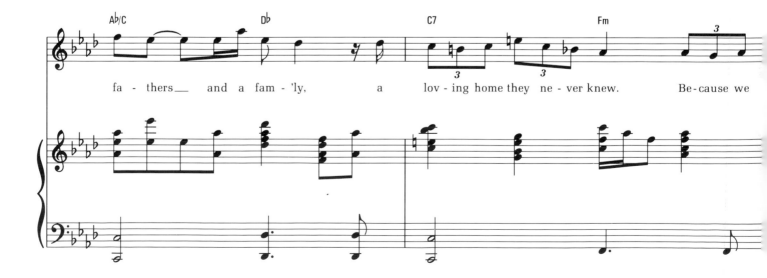

fa - thers and a fam - 'ly, a lov - ing home they ne - ver knew. Be-cause we

know   deep in our hearts___ that they are   all   our___ chil-dren   too.

These are souls   in   need,   they need us   to   give.

mp   *cresc.*

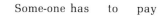

Some-one has to pay   for their chance to   live.

71

all the good we failed to do._____ Unis. Men That's why we know_____

all the good we failed to do._____ That's why we know_____ deep in our

all the good we failed to do._____ That's why we...

deep in our hearts____ that they are all our chil-dren too._____

hearts,__ that's why we know. Ah._____

Ah._____

Now That I've Seen Her

Music by Claude-Michel Schönberg
Lyrics by Richard Maltby Jr. & Alain Boublil

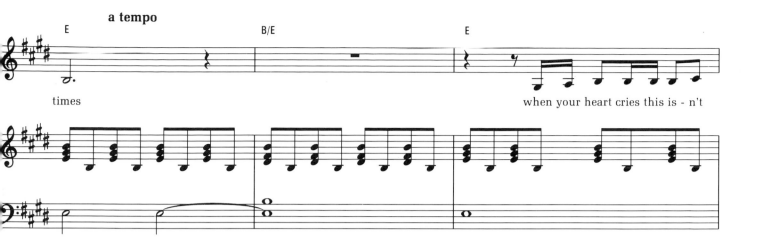

times ... when your heart cries this is - n't

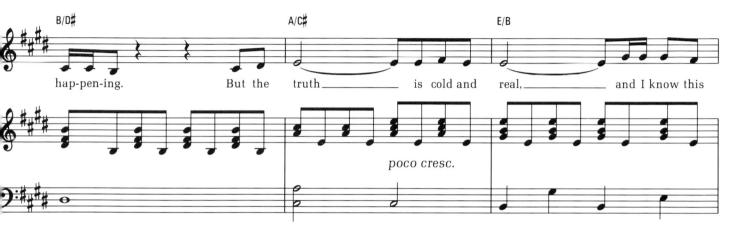

hap-pen-ing. But the truth____ is cold and real,____ and I know this

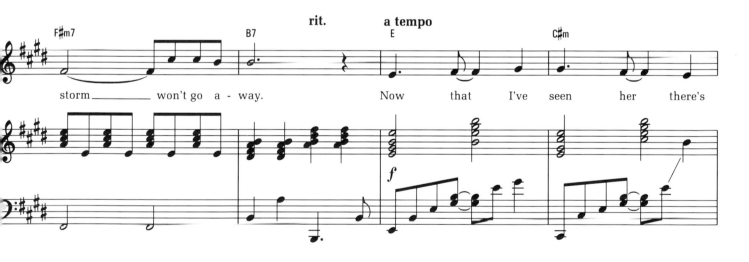

storm____ won't go a - way. Now that I've seen her there's

no way_ to hide, she is not some fling from long a - go.

Now that I've seen her I know why he lied, and I think it was

bet-ter when I did - n't know. _____ In her

eyes, in her voice, in the

heat ___ that filled the air part of him ___ still lin-gers there.

I know what pain her life to-day must be. But if it all comes down to

her or me, I won't wait, I___ swear_____ I'll fight.

Now that I've seen her she's

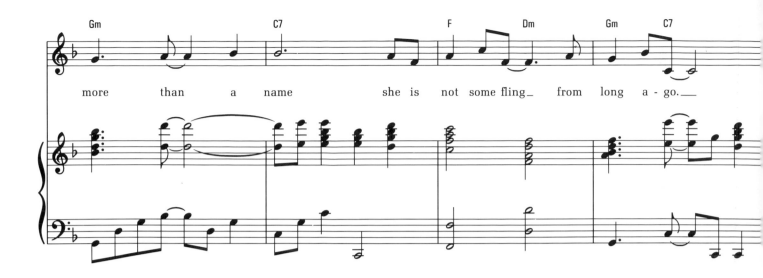

more than a name she is not some fling_ from long a-go._

Now that I've seen her I can't stay the same. Who's the man that I

al-ways trust-ed. Now I have to know._

The American Dream

Music by Claude-Michel Schönberg
Lyrics by Richard Maltby Jr. & Alain Boublil
Adapted from original French Lyrics by Alain Boublil

Make me Yan - kee,___ they're my fam - i - ly.___ They're sel - ling what peo - ple

a tempo

need. What's that I smell in the air,___ the A-mer - i - can dream

Sweet as a new mil-lion - aire,___ the A-mer - i - can dream.

Pre - packed and rea - dy to wear.

_ the A-mer - i-can dream._

Fat, like a choc'-late e - clair_ when you suck out the cream._

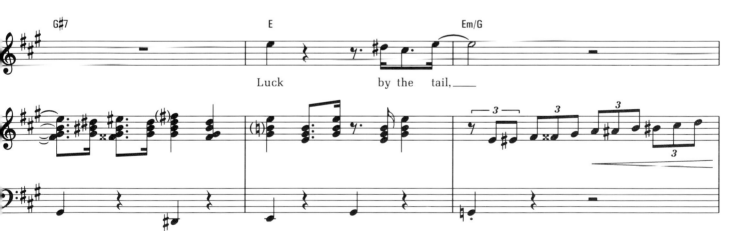

Luck by the tail,_

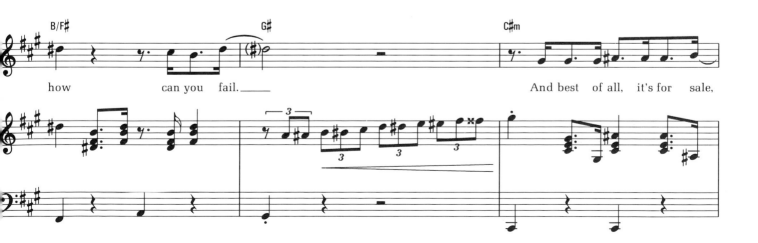

how can you fail._ And best of all, it's for sale,

the A-mer - i-can dream. _

Grea-sy drinks make life so slea - zy. _ In the States I'll build a

club that's four- starred. Men like me_ there have things ea - sy,_

they have a law - yer and a bo-dy-_ guard. To the johns there

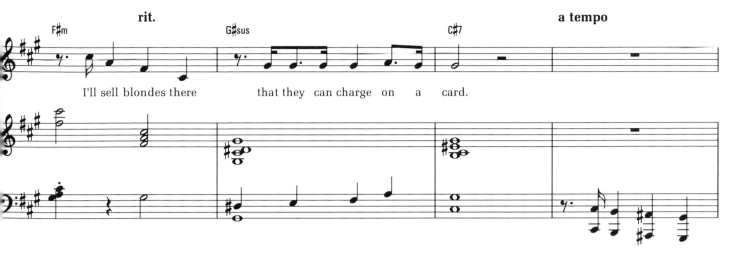

I'll sell blondes there that they can charge on a card.

What's that I smell in the air,____ the A-mer-i-can dream.

Sweet as a suite in Bel- air,____ the A-mer-i-can dream.

____ Girls can buy tits by the pair,

the A-mer - i - can dream.

Bald peo - ple think they'll grow hair,___ the A-mer - i - can dream

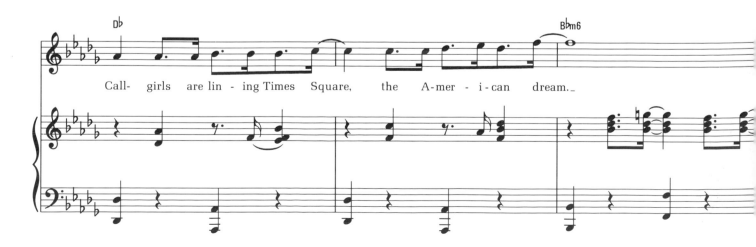

Call- girls are lin - ing Times Square, the A-mer - i - can dream.___

Bums there have mo - ney to spare,___ the A - mer - i - can dream.

___ Cars that have bars take you there,

___ the A - mer - i - can dream.

On stage each night Fred As - taire,

___ the A - mer - i - can dream.

Schlitz down the drain,

pop the cham-pagne,

it's time we all en-ter-tain__ my A-mer-i-can dream.__

Bus- boys can buy the ho- te

— the A-mer - i-can dream.

Wall street is rea - dy to sell,___ the A-mer - i-can dream.

Come make a life from thin air,___ the A-mer - i-can dream.

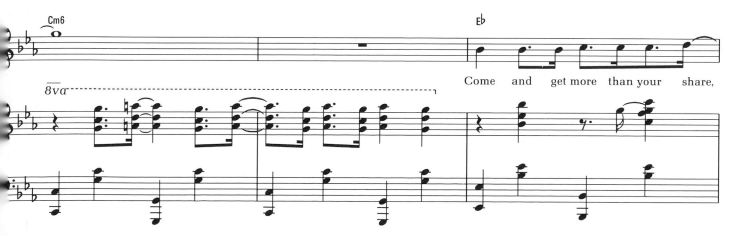

Come and get more than your share,

the A-mer-i-can dream. There I will crow

Miss Chi-na-town.

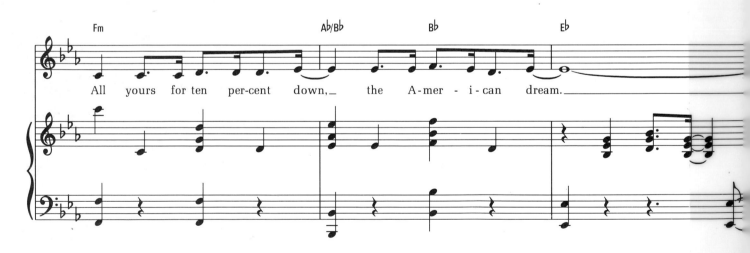

All yours for ten per-cent down,_ the A-mer-i-can dream.